GW00839031

The Complete Air Fryer Cookbook For Beginners

Recipes To Suit Every Occasion And All Meals Of The Day incl. Nutritions and Shopping List

Amber Garfield

Copyright © [2022] [Amber Garfield]

All rights reserved

All rights for this book here presented belong exclusively to the author. Usage or reproduction of the text is forbidden and requires a clear consent of the author in case of expectations.

ISBN - 9798354789023

Table of Contents

EXCLUSIVE BONUS

40 Weight Loss Recipes

&

14 Days Meal Plan

Scan the QR-Code and receive
the FREE download:

Amber Garfield

Introduction

Anyone who has an air fryer probably finds that they occasionally stare at it, unsure what they should make, but an air fryer is an enormously versatile gadget and you can make a whole range of different foods – both sweet and savoury – in your air fryer. You don't have to be an amazing chef to create some delicious and healthy recipes in your air fryer. Let's start with a quick look at what makes this gadget so great, how you use and maintain it, and why it's good for cooking healthy foods. We'll also cover some tips and tricks that will help you get the most from your fryer.

What Is An Air Fryer?

An air fryer might look a bit like one of those counter-top gadgets that rarely get used and only have one function, like a waffle maker or a toastie maker. However, an air fryer is a lot closer to your standard oven, and it's far more versatile than most of the other counter-top machines. Despite the name, it isn't really like a frying pan, and the food it creates is not quite "fried" in the traditional sense. You do not pour oil over it and heat it from below.

Instead, you spray the food or very lightly coat it in oil, and then place it in what is essentially an extremely hot miniature oven, where the heat circulates over and around the food, raising the temperature of the oil and "frying" the food. In general, this kind of food is actually a little more like baked food, but it is extremely tasty and is often seen as an excellent substitute for actual fried food – and it's a lot healthier.

Your food will brown nicely in the air fryer as the hot air conveys heat to the food and cooks it, just as it would in an oven. The air fryer has an open-weave metal basket that the food sits in, maximising the airflow and ensuring that all the food gets exposed to the heat.

You may occasionally need to toss the basket a bit to redistribute the food and allow the air to flow over all parts of it, but in general, air frying is a hands-off method of cooking that requires minimal attention while the food is cooking. It is also pretty quick, because it involves high temperatures, so you can have a meal ready in under an hour in most cases.

One of the big advantages of an air fryer is that you can put frozen foods in it without needing to thaw them first. Because the air fryer reaches high temperatures, there is no risk of bacteria growing on the outsides of the food before the inside is cooked, and this makes it ideal for the moments in which you have forgotten to get something out of the freezer in time.

Overall, however, most people opt to use their air fryer because it is considered much healthier than eating standard fried food. Things like chips / fries, nuggets, chicken wings, fried fish, and more can be made in an air fryer, and will taste pretty much as they would if they were deep fried in oil. This makes an air fryer an attractive option for anyone looking to reduce the amount of fat in their diet and boost their health and wellness.

It should be noted that an air fryer is generally considered "healthier," rather than "healthy," because it does still involve using oil. However, the amounts are massively decreased, and if you choose with care, you can make some pretty healthy meals in there – or enjoy a treat with far less guilt on your plate. Perhaps one of the biggest advantages is that you will waste a lot less oil when you cook using an air fryer. This means you'll be saving money and reducing food waste, and you won't have to deal with large quantities of used cooking oil that is difficult to recycle or reuse in any meaningful way.

How Do You Use An Air Fryer?

You will usually be using the metal basket that comes with your air fryer. Foods should be coated lightly in oil, and most people prefer to use a spray oil because this provides the thinnest possible coating. Avoid aerosol oils, however. You can also brush foods with oil, or lightly toss them.

You need to make sure you are using an oil with a high smoke point, such as peanut oil, so that your food doesn't get ruined by burnt oil. Because air fryers have such high cooking temperatures, the smoke point is significant, and you are at risk of ruining your whole meal and creating a terrible smell in your kitchen if you use an oil with a low smoke point.

Once you have prepared your food and oiled it, it should be placed in the basket, in a way that maximises the airflow. You need to make sure that you do not overfill the basket, or your food will end up soggy or even undercooked; without proper airflow, it cannot crisp up as it should. Most baskets should only be filled to the halfway mark, as this allows for proper cooking. Bear this in mind when choosing your air fryer and deciding what size of the device you need.

The air fryer then needs to be preheated before you add the food; this should not take long, but it does make a big difference to the overall flavour, so take the time to do it. Once the fryer is ready, the basket can be placed inside and the food will start to cook. Many recipes recommend taking it out and shaking it partway through, and this is generally not a problem with an air fryer. They do not lose heat when opened the way that a conventional oven would.

The food should then be given the allotted amount of time according to the recipe, and taken out. You should test meat with a thermometer to ensure that it has reached the correct temperature, and make sure that vegetables are cooked to your liking before you serve the meal.

What Are The Disadvantages Of An Air Fryer?

Air fryers do have a couple of disadvantages compared with traditional frying. For starters, you cannot cook battered foods like onion rings very easily, as the batter will drip through the holes in the basket and smoke when it hits the bottom. Foods like doughnuts are also pretty challenging to cook in an air fryer.

The other disadvantages include the fact that you have to store another gadget that takes up a fairly significant amount of space on the counter. Air fryers are bulky, especially if you want one that will cook a meal for more than 1-2 people, so you need to commit kitchen space if you want to own one.

Air fryers are also more limited when you want to make large amounts of food. You cannot simply add an extra pan to your hob; you only have the air fryer basket, and this is generally quite limited. You will have to cook food in batches, which means keeping it hot in the oven, which is less convenient than serving a whole batch of fried food at once.

How Do You Maintain An Air Fryer?

Air fryers need regular cleaning if they are not going to smell bad. A lot of people find that over time, their air fryer starts to take on a strange odour, or even produce smoke. This can be highly unappetizing and if you want to cook a batch of food, you should always stop if the fryer smells bad when you start.

To avoid this sort of thing, you should do both a regular clean and a semi-regular deep clean. After every use, allow your air fryer to fully cool (you can do this while you eat your meal) and then place all of the removable, washable components in soapy water to wash. Some are dishwasher safe, but it's always important to check this, and many people prefer to wash the components anyway because this can help to preserve the non-stick coating.

You should use a soft cloth to wash the components, and never scrub at them with a scourer or anything metal; this will ruin the coating. If food has got stuck to any of the components, leave them to soak for 20 minutes and then try again.

Do not put the main machine in water at any point. Instead, use a damp, soapy cloth to wipe out the inside once it is cool, and to remove any splashes of food from the front. This should get rid of any residue that has fallen from the basket, which might otherwise smoke the next time you use the machine.

To do a deep clean, you can use a toothbrush or toothpick to clean the inside of the machine, flicking crumbs out of the crevices and generally wiping down the insides of the air fryer. Wash all of the removable components well and leave them to dry before reassembling the machine. You should do this about once a month (or more often if you use the air fryer a lot), or if the machine starts to smell bad.

 Amber Garfield

Why Is Air Fryer Food Good For You?

A lot of people say that air fryer food is good for you, but this isn't strictly true. Air fryer food is only good for you if you are either swapping from a diet that is heavy in fried food (and this can be used as a transition step toward healthier options), or if you choose specifically healthy foods. Air fried vegetables can be pretty healthy, as minimal oil is used in cooking them, but if you eat a lot of battered meats, you may find that you aren't really following a healthy diet.

There is a temptation to assume that because it is air fried, it is okay, but you should be wary of this. A chip / fry is never going to be truly healthy, no matter what, although it is fine to eat them as part of a balanced diet. Be cautious about thinking of your air fryer as a healthy option, and make sure that your recipe choices are genuinely healthy.

Top Tips And Tricks For Your Air Fryer

Before we start looking at the many amazing meals you can make in your air fryer, let's cover a few great tips for making the most of this gadget. An air fryer can create some truly wonderful food if you use it correctly, so bear these suggestions in mind as you start experimenting.

Tip 1: Don't Overcrowd The Basket

We mentioned above that overcrowding the basket can stop your food from cooking properly, so it's important to avoid doing this. If you fill your air fryer's basket to more than halfway, you are likely to find that you get soggy food that lacks the crispiness most people are looking for when they fry. Unless you like damp, half-cooked vegetables and cold meat, it's crucial to avoid putting too much food in your air fryer.

The basket should never be more than halfway full, even if there are gaps among the pieces of food. If that means you have to cook in batches, do so, because otherwise your food will not taste very good. You can keep the food hot in the oven while you wait for further batches to finish cooking.

Tip 2: Oil Foods Properly

You might be tempted to try cutting out the oil entirely, but this isn't a good idea for many foods and it won't make your meal taste nice. The oil is responsible for making the food go crispy on the outside, and if you leave it off, you'll be missing that delicious crunchiness that makes fried foods so irresistible. A lot of people use spray oils so that they can keep the coating thin, but check the additives before doing this, and remember that these oils tend to be more expensive, and can damage your air fryer because of the agents that are used in them. Overall, it is best to just toss your foods in oil, or to invest in an oil mister that you can add oil to yourself.

You can lightly coat your food in oil before you start frying, and some recipes will call for a second coat once the food has begun cooking. This will increase the crispiness, but does bump up the oil content – although it is still nowhere near as fatty as traditional deep fried foods.

Note that the fattier the food itself is, the less oil you will need to add, and for some foods, you will find that you can get away with almost no oil, or none. For example, fatty cuts of meat can be air fried without any additional oil, and should still turn deliciously crispy in the fryer. For vegetables and low-fat foods, however, oil will be needed.

Tip 3: Give The Air Fryer Space

It's okay to push your air fryer into a corner out of the way when you aren't using it, but as soon as you want to cook, it needs to be away from the wall so that the air can circulate properly. Put at least 5 inches of space between the air fryer and the surrounding surfaces. It's especially important to keep the exhaust vent clear. This ensures the fryer can operate effectively and the food cooks well.

Tip 4: Preheat The Air Fryer

Many people think that preheating is a waste of time, and with a traditional oven, there are foods that don't require preheating. However, with an air fryer, you should almost always take the time to preheat it. This only takes a few minutes and it ensures that the food comes out deliciously crispy and evenly cooked every time. Some air fryers have a preheat option, but for others, you can just turn them on 2 or 3 minutes before you add the food.

Tip 5: Shake The Basket

Even if you spread your food out well when you first add it to the basket, pieces will be touching other pieces, and the air cannot circulate between them. Taking the basket out halfway through the cooking process and giving it a shake to redistribute the contents is more work, but it is a great way to ensure that the food cooks evenly and gets crispy all over.

You can do this more often for some foods, like French fries or chicken wings, which really want to be crispy. You may not mind so much with other foods. Large pieces can be flipped with tongs once or twice while cooking.

Tip 6: Use Oil When Seasoning

If you're used to just sprinkling herbs and spices on your foods and putting them in the oven, you might be planning to do the same when air frying – but you might need to take a slightly different approach. If you just put the spices straight on the food, you will find that the air fryer tends to blow them off and they fly around inside the machine instead. This is because there's a strong air current inside the fryer.

You should instead either mix the spices with oil before you coat the food, or oil the food and then sprinkle the herbs and spices on and rub them in. This will ensure that they stick well and the food soaks up the flavour.

Hopefully, you're now itching to learn some great recipes that will help you to make the most of your air fryer and turn you into a kitchen master. Bear the tips in mind as you work your way through the recipes below, so you can maximise your result every time you cook.

EXCLUSIVE BONUS

40 Weight Loss Recipes

&

14 Days Meal Plan

Scan the QR-Code and receive
the FREE download:

Amber Garfield

Delicious Meat & Fish Recipes

||||||||||||||||||||||||||||||||||||||||||||||||||||||||||||||||||||||||||||||||||||||||||||

Your air fryer can create incredible meat and fish, so don't limit it to fried vegetables and things like chips / fries; it can be so much more! You may not think of an air fryer creating phenomenal crispy salmon, luxurious fried shrimp, or superior pork chops, but it can do all of these things and more, so don't underestimate it. Some people view an air fryer as a gadget for making cheap and cheerful fast food, but in fact, it can create some incredibly high end and delicious meals that you'd never know were cooked in a little gadget on the counter. So, let's explore some!

Air Fried Lemon Shrimps

Air fried shrimps are succulent, rich, and delightfully crispy, and they're the perfect way to lend a meal an extra touch of class. Whether you stir them into a pasta dish, serve them as a side, or use them to top a particularly delicious salad, air fried shrimps are a sure win for all occasions.

SERVES: 4

You will need:

- 450 g / 1 lb of raw shrimp, peeled and deveined
- 2 tablespoons of lemon juice
- 120 ml / 1/2 cup of olive oil
- 1/2 teaspoon of salt
- 1 teaspoon of black pepper
- 1 small clove of garlic

Amber Garfield

1 Juice your lemon and crush the garlic into a fine mince. Mix the garlic into the lemon juice, along with the olive oil, pepper, and salt, and pour the mixture into a Ziploc bag.

2 Preheat your air fryer to 205 degrees C / 400 degrees F.

3 Add the shrimps to the Ziploc bag, seal the top, and shake to combine. You can let the shrimps stand for a few minutes so that they absorb more flavours if you like, or simply move on to the cooking stage.

4 Cut a piece of parchment paper to fit in the bottom of your air fryer basket, and then take the shrimps out of the lemon mix and place them in a single layer at the bottom of the basket.

5 Put the basket in the air fryer and cook it for around 4 minutes. Take the basket out and shake it, or use tongs to turn the shrimps over, and then put the basket back and cook for another 4 minutes.

6 Take the shrimps out and inspect them. The shells should have turned pink, while the shrimps will have gone slightly white, and opaque. They may also have some slightly golden edges. If they look undercooked, give them another minute.

7 Take the shrimps out of the air fryer and toss them back into the lemon juice, and then serve with whatever other ingredients you desire. They can be stirred through 225 g / 8 oz of cooked pasta if you like, or added to a salad.

Nutritional info (not including pasta/other accompaniments):

Calories: 354

Fat: 27.2 g

Cholesterol: 239 mg

Sodium: 569 mg

Carbohydrates: 2.2 g

Fibre: 0.2 g

Protein: 26 g

Air Fried White Fish

If you love the kind of fish that you can buy from your local chip shop, you might be wondering whether you can reproduce this in your air fryer, and the great news is that you can – and it only takes about 20 minutes! This recipe will be popular with kids and adults alike, and gives you access to a traditional meal that many people love. Serve it with peas or sweetcorn and boiled potatoes or mash.

SERVES: 4

You will need:

- ¹/₂ tablespoon of olive oil
- 400 g / 14 oz of fish fillets (or 4 fish fillets of a size that suits your family)
- 50 g / ¹/₂ cup of breadcrumbs
- Pinch of paprika
- Pinch of chilli powder
- ¹/₄ teaspoon of salt
- Pinch of black pepper
- Pinch of garlic powder
- Pinch of onion powder

Method:

1. Defrost your fish fillets before you start. This isn't necessary for air frying usually, but frozen fish may make your breadcrumbs go soggy before they have had a chance to cook, so it's best to thaw it out. You can do this in the microwave, or by placing it in the fridge 24 hours before you want to cook it.

2. Take a shallow bowl and mix together the breadcrumbs and all of the spices listed above. You can adjust the quantities of any of the spices if you like to make the meal suit your tastes.

3. Preheat your air fryer to 200 degrees C / 390 degrees F.

4. Roll each fillet in the breadcrumbs until it is thoroughly coated, and then place it in the air fryer basket, leaving room between each one. If your air fryer is small, cook the fillets in batches.

5. Cook for around 9 minutes and then take the basket out and flip each fillet over.

6. Cook for another 5-6 minutes, so that the breadcrumbs are thoroughly crispy and delicious. Check that the fish is hot through before serving.

Amber Garfield

Nutritional info:

Calories: 142

Fat: 2.5 g

Cholesterol: 0 mg

Sodium: 247 mg

Carbohydrates: 10 g

Fibre: 0.7 g

Protein: 17.9 g

Air Fried Succulent Pork Chops

Pork chops are a super popular meal, and they're also very easy to make in your air fryer. They take less than half an hour, and you'll find that they stay deliciously succulent and rich. You would never know that they hadn't been grilled, and this is a low mess option for making these without getting meat fat all over your kitchen.

SERVES: 4

You will need:

- 4 pork chops (boneless)
- 2 teaspoons of vegetable oil
- 1/2 teaspoon of celery seed
- 1/2 teaspoon of chopped parsley
- 1 clove of garlic
- Pinch of salt
- 1/4 teaspoon of sugar
- 1/2 teaspoon of onion powder

Method:

1 Start by peeling and mincing the garlic finely, and then add it to a shallow dish.

2 Preheat your air fryer to 175 degrees C / 350 degrees F.

3 Add the rest of the seasoning, and place the pork chops in the dish. Roll them over to coat them in seasoning, and then oil the pork chops and massage the oil in.

4 Place the chops in the air fryer basket with some space in between them.

5 Cook the pork chops for 5 minutes if they are thin, and 8 minutes if they are thick. Take them out and turn them over using tongs, and then put them back in the air fryer.

6 Cook for another 5 or 8 minutes, and then check whether they have reached the desired temperature. 62 degrees C / 145 degrees F is the minimum safe temperature for pork chops, but you may want to cook them more if you prefer well done pork – up to around 71 degrees C / 160 degrees F.

7 Serve sizzling hot with whatever side dishes you prefer.

Nutritional info:

Calories: 244

Fat: 15.3 g

Cholesterol: 55 mg

Sodium: 731 mg

Carbohydrates: 1.8 g

Fibre: 0.1 g

Protein: 25.1 g

Amber Garfield

Air Fried Chicken Wings

If you have an air fryer, you're not putting it to good use unless you occasionally create some golden chicken wings in it. You can make them just as delicious as deep fried chicken wings, with a fraction of the fat, and all the flavour. This is a great way to make your air fryer beloved by the whole family, especially the kids, and you can really cater to a party if you're organised and you've got a hot oven nearby to keep the batches toasty while you make more.

SERVES: 2

You will need:

- 12 chicken wings (to serve 6 each to 2 people)
- 1 teaspoon of granulated garlic
- 1/2 teaspoon of salt
- 1/2 teaspoon of baking powder
- 1 tablespoon of chilli powder

Method:

1 Place the chicken wings on some paper towels and dry them thoroughly. You want to get them as dry as you can before you season them, because this will give you the crispiest exterior possible, so take your time over this.

2 Preheat your air fryer to 210 degrees C / 410 degrees F.

3 Toss your chicken wings into the spices and rub them in to ensure all parts of the wings are covered.

4 Oil the basket of your air fryer to reduce any risk of sticking. You are not oiling the chicken, so it's important to increase the non-stick properties of the basket.

5 Place the chicken wings in the basket, spacing them out so that the air can flow over them.

6 Cook the chicken wings for 10 minutes, and then take the basket out and use tongs to turn them and shake them around.

7 Cook for a further 12 minutes, and then check whether they are crispy enough. If you want them crispier, turn them again and put them back for a few more minutes.

8 Keep them hot in the oven while waiting for the next batch to finish if you are making large quantities.

Amber Garfield

Nutritional info:

Calories: 973

Fat: 64.8 g

Cholesterol: 232 mg

Sodium: 1564 mg

Carbohydrates: 37 g

Fibre: 2.4 g

Protein: 59.1 g

Lamb Burgers In The Air Fryer

Lamb is often an under-utilised meat, but this isn't because it lacks flavour or texture. Many people love it, but aren't quite sure how to cook it unless they're making a Sunday roast – so why not try these delicious lamb burgers in your air fryer? They are easy to make and you can again whip them up in under half an hour, making them ideal for busy weeknight dinners.

SERVES: 4

You will need:

- 1/3 white onion
- 1 clove of garlic
- Pinch of salt
- 480 g / 1 lb. of ground lamb
- Pinch of black pepper
- 2 teaspoons of olive oil

Amber Garfield

Method:

1 Peel and chop your onion and garlic.

2 Place a skillet over a medium heat and add the onion. Cook gently for about 4 minutes, until brown and starting to soften.

3 Add the garlic and cook for 1 minute more.

4 Place the ingredients in a bowl and add the ground lamb to the bowl. Stir thoroughly.

5 Preheat your air fryer to 200 degrees C / 400 degrees F, and then lower the temperature to 185 degrees C / 375 degrees F for cooking.

6 Shape the lamb into 3 burgers, using a burger press if you have one, and place them in the air fryer basket. Fry for 8 minutes and then take them out, turn them, and fry them for another 8 minutes.

7 Serve hot with bread rolls or boiled potatoes.

Nutritional info:

Calories: 411

Fat: 32.8 g

Cholesterol: 108 mg

Sodium: 476 mg

Carbohydrates: 1.5 g

Fibre: 0.3 g

Protein: 25.8 g

Amber Garfield

Air Fryer Desserts

Many people think that their air fryer is great for making dinners, lunches, and side dishes, but few people remember that they can make some pretty incredible desserts in the air fryer. The oversight may be because we aren't used to "frying" desserts, but remember that your air fryer is more like an oven than a frying pan, and that means you can make some delicious treats in it if you get a little more imaginative. These may not be the best way to maintain your healthy streak, but they are fun and can be a great way to use your air fryer more.

Air Fryer Chocolate Chip Cookies

There's not much that can beat a chocolate chip cookie, and if you're a big fan of these popular treats, you'll be glad to know that they are pretty easy to make in the air fryer. Whether you're making them for a birthday party, lunch box desserts, or just for general enjoyment, you can whip up a batch in under an hour, and it's very easy.

SERVES: 12 COOKIES

You will need:

- 115 g / ½ cup of butter
- 50 g / ¼ cup of brown sugar
- 50 g / ¼ cup of white sugar
- Pinch of salt
- 1 large egg
- 1 teaspoon of vanilla extract
- ½ teaspoon of baking soda
- 130 g / 1 ½ cups of flour
- 120 g / ¾ cup of chocolate chips
- 35 g / 1/3 cup of chopped walnuts

Amber Garfield

Method:

1. Preheat your air fryer to 175 degrees C / 350 degrees F.

2. Melt the butter in a small pan or in the microwave.

3. Take out a medium bowl and add the melted butter and both kinds of sugar.

4. Add the egg and the vanilla extract, and then whisk all of the ingredients together until combined.

5. Sift in the flour, followed by the baking soda and salt. Stir well.

6. Cut a piece of parchment paper that will fit in the bottom of your air fryer basket, and put it in place, making sure that the air can flow around the edges.

7. Take a teaspoon or a cookie scoop and scoop dough onto the paper, leaving around 2-3 inches around each cookie. You will need to work in batches, depending on the size of your air fryer.

8. Bake the cookies for about 8 minutes. They should turn golden and soft. Lift them out of the air fryer and place them on the counter to cool. Allow them about 5 minutes to cool before serving them.

Nutritional info (per cookie):

Calories: 236

Fat: 13.3 g

Cholesterol: 36 mg

Sodium: 218 mg

Carbohydrates: 25.7 g

Fibre: 1 g

Protein: 3.8 g

Amber Garfield

Air Fried Churros

If you've ever had churros at a street fair, you will know just how deliciously crispy, tender, and delightful these treats can be. They aren't the easiest thing to make at home though – unless you have an air fryer. Because they usually require deep frying to get their golden, tempting dough, not many people make these at home, so yours will be a particularly sought after treat. You do need a pastry bag with a 1M tip, and the recipe is a bit more involved than some others, but worth the extra effort.

SERVES: 24 CHURROS

You will need:

- 120 g / ½ cup of milk
- 120 g / ½ cup of water
- 115 g / ½ cup of butter
- 120 g / 1 cup of flour
- 1 teaspoon of vanilla extract
- 3 eggs
- 200 g / 1 cup of sugar, with a tablespoon separated

Method:

1 Place a saucepan over a medium heat and add the milk and water, along with the butter and the tablespoon of sugar.

2 Bring the pan to a slow boil, stirring so that it doesn't stick.

3 Take the pan off the heat and place it on a heatproof mat. Stir in the flour, working slowly so that it doesn't form lumps.

4 When the flour has completely mixed in, place the pan back on the heat and keep stirring it for 2 minutes. It should start forming a ball.

5 Take the pan off the heat and move the dough into a mixing bowl. If you have an electric mixer, the next step will be faster, but you can do it by hand.

6 Beat the dough hard for 3-5 minutes (or longer if you are working by hand). It should start to turn fluffy. This will also help it to cool down; you don't want to add the eggs to a hot mixture or they will cook.

7 Take out a small bowl and mix together the eggs and vanilla, beating hard until frothy.

Amber Garfield

8 Check that your main mixture has cooled and then slowly add the egg mixture, beating thoroughly as you stir it. Pause to scrape the mixture down into the bowl every so often and keep mixing until you have a smooth dough.

9 Transfer your dough into a pastry bag with the tip in place, and preheat your air fryer to 190 degrees C / 380 degrees F.

10 Pipe the dough straight into the air fryer basket, using scissors or a sharp knife to sever the dough when you are happy with the length.

11 Use a mister bottle to lightly spray oil onto the churros, and then put the basket into the fryer and cook for around 8 minutes. Take them out and check whether they are golden. If they aren't, give them another couple of minutes in the fryer.

12 Tip the rest of the sugar into a bowl, along with any other spices that you fancy, such as cinnamon or nutmeg. When the churros come out of the fryer, toss them in the sugar and serve piping hot. You can add chocolate sauce if you choose.

Nutritional info (per churros):

Calories: 95

Fat: 4.5 g

Cholesterol: 31 mg

Sodium: 38 mg

Carbohydrates: 12.6 g

Fibre: 0.1 g

Protein: 1.4 g

Amber Garfield

Brownies

Brownies are one of the most popular and most loved recipes out there, and if you're going to any sort of dinner or bring-your-own event, you'll find they go down beautifully. They can be classy, but they are also wonderful for kids' parties. You can make a batch in your air fryer in around 40 minutes, and nobody will ever know that they weren't baked in the oven. If you love that crispy top, you'll find this method perfect.

SERVES: 2

You will need:

- 🍽 35 g / 1/3 cup of cocoa powder
- 🍽 1/4 teaspoon of baking powder
- 🍽 100 g / 1/2 cup sugar
- 🍽 30 g / 1/4 cup of flour
- 🍽 Pinch of salt
- 🍽 1 large egg
- 🍽 60 g / 1/4 cup of butter

1 Grease a cake tin that will fit into your air fryer. It ideally should be about 6 inches.

2 Take out a medium bowl and add the cocoa powder, baking powder, sugar, flour, and salt. Mix to combine.

3 Melt the butter and allow it to cool slightly, and then whisk in the egg.

4 Slowly tip the egg mixture into the dry mixture, stirring as you go to prevent lumps from forming.

5 Tip the batter into your cake tin and smooth the top down with a spatula.

6 Preheat your air fryer to 175 degrees C / 350 degrees F and bake the brownie for 16 minutes. Check whether it is done by inserting a toothpick into the centre, and cook for another couple of minutes if necessary.

7 Take the tin out of the air fryer and place it on the counter to cool for 10 minutes before serving.

Nutritional info:

Calories: 516

Fat: 27.5 g

Cholesterol: 154 mg

Sodium: 280 mg

Carbohydrates: 70.3 g

Fibre: 4.7 g

Protein: 7.6 g

Air Fried Baked Apples

If you fancy a healthier dessert, baked apples are a wonderful option that looks amazing and tastes even better. These will get even the kids enthusiastic, and they are easy to make. They take a little bit longer, at around an hour in total, but they are certainly worth it, and it's nice to find a dessert that uses some fruit. You can omit the ice cream from these if you'd like to make the recipe healthier, or add some chocolate sauce or caramel to make it even tastier.

SERVES: 4

You will need:

- 🍽 1 tablespoon of brown sugar
- 🍽 1 tablespoon of white sugar
- 🍽 ½ teaspoon of ground cinnamon
- 🍽 4 tablespoons of butter
- 🍽 4 apples
- 🍽 4 scoops of vanilla ice cream (or your choice of flavour)

Method:

1 Melt your butter in a small bowl, and then whisk in both kinds of sugar and the ground cinnamon.

2 Wash your apples and cut off the tops. Use a sharp knife to carefully cut out most of the core without slicing the rest of the apple. Don't cut out the very bottom of the core; this is going to hold the butter and cinnamon in place.

3 Next, hold the apple firmly and position the knife a few centimetres from the core. You are now going to make a slice that follows around the core, as though you were cutting out a second, larger core – but don't cut all the way through the flesh. Do this twice so that there are two circles cut in the top of the apple around the hole where you removed the core.

4 Next, turn the apple over so that the cut size is pressed against the chopping board. Make small cuts from the top to the bottom all around the apple, being careful not to cut any flesh away entirely. These slices will open up the apple and help the heat to spread through it, ensuring that it cooks more quickly. If you don't open the apple up, it will take a long time to cook and may burn on the outside before the inside is done.

5 Turn the apple back over and brush it all over with the melted butter and cinnamon mixture.

6 Preheat the air fryer to 175 degrees C / 350 degrees F and then place the apples in the air fryer basket with some room for the air to flow. Put the basket in the air fryer, and bake them for 15 minutes.

7 Take the apples out of the basket and light squeeze to see if they are tender and cooked. If they still feel too firm, put them back in the air fryer for 5 minutes.

8 Serve with vanilla ice cream scooped over the top.

Nutritional info:

Calories: 375

Fat: 18.9 g

Cholesterol: 60 mg

Sodium: 137 mg

Carbohydrates: 52.3 g

Fibre: 6.1 g

Protein: 3 g

Amber Garfield

Air Fried Lemon Cookies

If you loved the chocolate chip cookie recipe, you will find these mouth-wateringly good. They are light, citrusy, and perfect for an after supper snack. You can add a swirl of icing sugar once they are cooked, or keep them plain if you prefer your foods a little less sweet. Feel free to increase the quantity of lemon juice a little if you want it to have a sharper flavour.

SERVES: 12 COOKIES

You will need:

- 400 g / 2 cups of sugar
- 230 g / 1 cup of butter
- 2 eggs
- 1 teaspoon of vanilla extract
- 1 1/2 tablespoons of lemon juice
- 1 tablespoon of lemon zest
- 385 g / 3 cups of flour
- 1 1/4 teaspoons of baking powder
- 1/4 teaspoon of baking soda
- 1/2 teaspoon of salt

1. Take out a large bowl and cream the butter and the sugar for 4 minutes, until fluffy.

2. Add the eggs and vanilla and mix them in.

3. Zest and juice the lemon and stir the zest and juice into the mixture.

4. Preheat your air fryer to 175 degrees C / 350 degrees F.

5. Add the flour, baking soda, baking powder, and salt, and mix lightly until everything is combined. You should have a thick, stiff dough.

6. Line your air fryer basket with tin foil.

7. Roll the dough into small balls and place as many as will fit into your air fryer basket, leaving room between them so that they can spread and the air can flow.

8. Bake them for 5 minutes and then check on them. If they are ready, they will have set firm. They may take up to 7 minutes, depending on your air fryer.

9 Allow them to cool while you make the remaining batches. It may take several batches, especially if you only have a small air fryer. Do not crowd the cookies, or they will run into each other and form into one big cookie, which may not cook very well.

Nutritional info (per cookie):

Calories: 387

Fat: 16.4 g

Cholesterol: 68 mg

Sodium: 245 mg

Carbohydrates: 57.7 g

Fibre: 0.9 g

Protein: 4.3 g

Amber Garfield

Tasty Air Fryer Snacks

||||||||||||||||||||||||||||||||||||||||||||||||||||||||||||||||||||||||||||||||||||||||

If you are a big fan of snacks, you'll be pleased to learn that you can make some great snacks in your air fryer. It's flexible and because it cooks so quickly, you can have snacks for all the family without having to spend hours slaving away in the kitchen. Snacks are a great way to keep yourself topped up throughout the day, or can be served alongside a meal if you prefer.

Air Fried Spicy Avocado Wedges

Avocados are a great snack to enjoy, but if you're getting bored of eating them with oil and vinegar, you might enjoy these delightfully crispy wedges. If you want to make this treat vegan, you can substitute the egg for aquafaba, but otherwise, it's easier made with egg. If you don't enjoy spice, simply omit the chilli, or if you'd like them to be hotter, add a little more.

SERVES: 4

You will need:

- 1 avocado
- 50 g / ½ cup of breadcrumbs
- Pinch of salt
- 1 egg
- ½ teaspoon of chilli powder

Method:

1 Start by peeling and pitting your avocado, and then slice it into thin strips around ½ inch thick.

2 Take out a shallow bowl and crack the egg in, and then mix it up.

3 In a second bowl, mix the breadcrumbs, chilli, and salt together.

4 Preheat your air fryer to 200 degrees C / 390 degrees F.

5 Swipe each slice of avocado through the egg, and then through the breadcrumb mixture, coating both sides. If there are any gaps, pat a little more egg and breadcrumb into place so that the avocado is completely covered.

6 Arrange the slices in the bottom of the air fryer basket with no overlap, and then bake them for 20 minutes. You don't need to flip them, although you can if you want to.

Nutritional info:

Calories: 172

Fat: 11.6 g

Cholesterol: 41 mg

Sodium: 408 mg

Carbohydrates: 14.1 g

Fibre: 4 g

Protein: 4.1 g

Amber Garfield

Cinnamon Sweet Chips / Fries

If you'd like a sweeter snack, these chips / fries are usually a hit. They need to be eaten hot, but they make a wonderful treat for a weekend afternoon, or for a movie night. They are sugary and salty, and utterly delicious.

SERVES: 4

You will need:

- 2 sweet potatoes
- 2 tablespoons of butter, divided
- 2 tablespoons of white sugar
- 1/2 teaspoon of cinnamon

1 Wash your sweet potato and cut it into thin slices. You can remove the peel before slicing if you like, or leave it on; it will turn crispy and delicious.

2 Preheat your air fryer to 190 degrees C / 380 degrees F.

3 Melt the butter and scoop 1 tablespoon over the fries, tossing to coat them.

4 Put the chips / fries in the basket. It's fine to let the fries touch, but don't fill the basket too full, or they won't crisp up properly.

5 Fry them for 10 minutes, and then take the basket out and shake it thoroughly. Put them back in and fry for another 5-8 minutes.

6 Put them on a plate and sprinkle them with sugar and cinnamon, and the remaining butter. Mix to coat the chips / fries, and enjoy hot.

Nutritional info:

Calories: 124

Fat: 5.8 g

Cholesterol: 15 mg

Sodium: 76 mg

Carbohydrates: 17.7 g

Fibre: 2.2 g

Protein: 1.1 g

Cornbread

Cornbread makes a wonderful snack, with a delicious, soft, buttery flavour. It's easy to make, especially if you have some silicone muffin cases that can be used in your air fryer. You can also use any square pan that will fit into your air fryer. This only takes about 20 minutes to make, and it's a food you can snack on any time!

SERVES: 8

You will need:

- 120 g / ¾ cup of cornmeal
- 1 teaspoon of baking powder
- Pinch of salt
- 155 g / 1 ¼ cups of flour
- 3 tablespoons of sugar
- 1 large egg
- 55 g / ¼ cup of melted butter
- 240 ml / 1 cup of buttermilk

Method:

1 Get out a medium bowl and then sift together the cornmeal, baking powder, salt, flour, and sugar.

2 Melt the butter and add it to the bowl, followed by the egg and buttermilk. Stir the ingredients together until they form a thick batter.

3 Preheat your air fryer to 175 degrees C / 350 degrees F.

4 Pour the batter into the baking dish or silicone cups, leaving a bit of room at the top.

5 Place the tin or cups in the air fryer basket, and then cook for 14 minutes. Use a toothpick to test whether the cornbread is cooked through, and make sure it is golden brown before serving.

Nutritional info:

Calories: 202

Fat: 7.2 g

Cholesterol: 40 mg

Sodium: 160 mg

Carbohydrates: 30 g

Fibre: 1.4 g

Protein: 4.8 g

Amber Garfield

Air Fried Vegetables

||||||||||||||||||||||||||||||||||||||||||||||||||||||||||||||||||||||||||||||||||

If you're trying to increase the number of vegetables that you eat, you might find that your air fryer is a great way to make delicious, crispy, tempting vegetables quickly and easily. It can be a challenge to get more vegetables into your diet, but fried vegetables can be particularly tasty, and they are easy to eat, so they make great side dishes or just snacks.

Parmesan Air Fryer Carrots

If you love carrots, you're in for a real treat with these delicious, crispy, cheesy carrots. These work well as a side dish, or you can make them your main meal if you just want something light. They are simple and healthy, and they only take about a quarter of an hour to make.

SERVES: 4

You will need:

- 🍽 6 carrots
- 🍽 60 ml / ¼ cup of olive oil
- 🍽 ½ teaspoon of parsley
- 🍽 ½ teaspoon of oregano
- 🍽 ½ teaspoon of garlic powder
- 🍽 2 tablespoons of Parmesan
- 🍽 Pinch of salt
- 🍽 Pinch of pepper

Amber Garfield

Method:

1. Wash, peel, and slice your carrots into small chunks.

2. Take out a small bowl and add the oil, Parmesan, herbs, garlic powder, pepper, and salt.

3. Toss the carrots into the oil and swirl them around until they are fully coated.

4. Place them in the air fryer basket and cook them at 180 degrees C / 360 degrees F for 10 minutes, or up to 12 minutes if you'd like them to be really crispy.

Nutritional info:

Calories: 170

Fat: 14.1 g

Cholesterol: 5 mg

Sodium: 128 mg

Carbohydrates: 9.7 g

Fibre: 2.4 g

Protein: 3.1 g

Air Fried Brussels Sprouts With Lemon

Brussels sprouts are the enemy of small children, but if you cook them up in your air fryer, they are like an entirely different vegetable. They become sweet, crispy, nutty, and moreish. You can add any other herbs or spices that you like to these, adapting this simple recipe if you prefer a stronger taste.

SERVES: 4

You will need:

- 🍽 450 g / 1 lb of Brussels sprouts
- 🍽 2 teaspoons of olive oil
- 🍽 Pinch of salt
- 🍽 Pinch of black pepper
- 🍽 3 cloves of garlic
- 🍽 2 tablespoons of lemon juice

Method:

1. Prepare your Brussels sprouts for cooking by trimming off the ends, removing any tough or yellow leaves, and washing them. Cut them in half, and cut any particularly large sprouts into quarters so that they can cook properly.

2. Preheat your air fryer to 190 degrees C / 375 degrees F.

3. Pat the sprouts dry and place them in a bowl. Drizzle the olive oil across them, along with the salt, pepper, and any spices that appeal to you.

4. Peel your garlic cloves and slice them thinly. Set the slices aside for now.

5. Toss the sprouts to coat them in oil, and then add them to the air fryer basket.

6. Cook them for 5 minutes, and then take the basket out and shake it. Toss the sprouts around and put them back in for 5 more minutes. If they look like they are almost ready, add the sliced garlic and toss the sprouts again. Put them back in for another 3 minutes to allow the garlic to cook, and the sprouts to become rich and crispy.

7. Serve the sprouts hot and drizzle the lemon juice across them. If you don't like lemon, consider a swirl of honey, some chilli sauce, or a pinch of nutmeg.

Nutritional info:

Calories: 74

Fat: 2.8 g

Cholesterol: 0 mg

Sodium: 178 mg

Carbohydrates: 11.3 g

Fibre: 4.4 g

Protein: 4.1 g

Amber Garfield

Air Fried Roast Potatoes

Anyone who regularly makes Sunday dinners will know the ongoing battle to create the perfect roasted potato – and your air fryer can help here. If you find that you've never got enough space in the oven and you're always fighting for more room, moving the potatoes to the air fryer is an even bigger bonus, and you'll get absolutely delicious, perfectly crispy potatoes every time. You don't need to do any par-boiling, either, minimising the need for extra pans and more washing up.

SERVES: 4

You will need:

- 🍽 2 tablespoons of olive oil
- 🍽 ½ teaspoon of paprika
- 🍽 ½ teaspoon of garlic powder
- 🍽 ½ teaspoon of salt
- 🍽 Pinch of pepper
- 🍽 680 g / 1 ½ g of potatoes

Method:

1 Take out a large bowl and add the oil, garlic powder, paprika, pepper, and salt.

2 Preheat your air fryer to 195 degrees C / 380 degrees F.

3 Wash the potatoes and peel them if you like, and then pat them dry and toss them in the oil. Make sure they are thoroughly coated; this will ensure that they get a crispy exterior.

4 Put the potatoes into the air fryer and roast them for 10 minutes. Take them out and flip them over. You might find it easier to tip them out of the basket and then toss them back in to ensure that they are all turned over.

5 Roast them for 10 minutes more, and then serve with extra salt and pepper if desired.

Nutritional info:

Calories: 180

Fat: 7.2 g

Cholesterol: 0 mg

Sodium: 448 mg

Carbohydrates: 27.2 g

Fibre: 4.2 g

Protein: 3 g

Crispy Cauliflower Florets

Cauliflower is a vegetable that many people find a bit challenging, but it's packed with goodness and if you cook it right, it can be delicious. This is another recipe where you can change the herbs and spices to suit your tastes, and you'll still end up with crunchy, tempting cauliflower in less than half an hour. You can again use this dish as a side, or snack on the florets throughout the day.

SERVES: 4

You will need:

- 🍽 1 cauliflower head
- 🍽 1 tablespoon of olive oil
- 🍽 ½ teaspoon of smoked paprika
- 🍽 ½ teaspoon of turmeric
- 🍽 ¼ teaspoon of salt
- 🍽 Pinch of black pepper

1 Wash the cauliflower and cut it into florets. Include the stems; there is no reason to waste these and they taste just as good as the heads.

2 Add the olive oil and the spices to a medium bowl, and toss the cauliflower florets in it until they are fully coated.

3 Preheat your air fryer to 200 degrees C / 390 degrees F and then roast the cauliflower in it for 3 minutes.

4 Take it out and flip it, and put it back for 3 more minutes. Repeat this process until around 15 minutes have passed and the cauliflower is crispy and tender. You can eat it hot or cold, so it makes a great snack for keeping in the fridge.

Nutritional info:

Calories: 48

Fat: 3.6 g

Cholesterol: 0 mg

Sodium: 167 mg

Carbohydrates: 3.8 g

Fibre: 1.8 g

Protein: 1.4 g

Amber Garfield

Air Fryer Main Dishes

||||||||||||||||||||||||||||||||||||||||||||||||||||||||||||||||||||||||||||||||||||||||||

Of course, your air fryer's true moment to shine is in the making of your main meals. You do sometimes need to juggle a bit, as air fryer baskets can be too small to easily cook a full main meal, but the food cooked in there is worth the extra effort, for sure! You can make some amazingly fancy and some very simple meals by air frying them.

Air Fryer Pork Tenderloin

Pork tenderloin is delicious and ideal if you are serving a fancy dinner, because you can't go wrong with this recipe. You can adjust the seasoning if you aren't sure about the quantities, or swap one spice for another, making this your own. The air fryer is the perfect way to get pork crispy on the outside and tender in the centre. You should use a meat thermometer to check that it has reached a minimum temperature of 62 degrees C / 145 degrees F before serving.

SERVES: 4

You will need:

- 560 g / 1 1/4 lb of pork tenderloin
- 1/2 tablespoon of olive oil
- 1 teaspoon of paprika
- 1/2 teaspoon of onion powder
- 1/2 teaspoon of cayenne pepper
- 1 1/2 teaspoons of salt
- 2 tablespoons of brown sugar
- 1 teaspoon of ground mustard
- 1/2 teaspoon of black pepper
- 1/4 teaspoon of garlic powder

Amber Garfield

Method:

1 Trim your pork tenderloin to remove any excess fat or silver skin.

2 Coat the tenderloin with the oil and rub it in well.

3 Preheat your air fryer to 200 degrees C / 400 degrees F.

4 Mix together all the dry ingredients and then rub them into the tenderloin.

5 Place the tenderloin in the air fryer and cook it for 20 minutes. Take it out and check the internal temperature is at least 62 degrees C / 145 degrees F. If not, cook it for another few minutes until it reaches the proper temperature. Don't serve the pork until it is hot enough.

6 When it has reached temperature, take it out and place it on a cutting board. Allow it to cool for 5 minutes before you cut into it. This ensures that the juices can redistribute themselves throughout the meat, and prevents it from being lost onto the cutting board. Spread any juices that do run out over the meat, and sprinkle on extra spices if desired.

Nutritional info:

Calories: 246

Fat: 7.2 g

Cholesterol: 103 mg

Sodium: 955 mg

Carbohydrates: 6.3 g

Fibre: 0.9 g

Protein: 37.7 g

Amber Garfield

Air Fryer Egg Fried Rice

Before you call for your favourite takeaway / takeout, get out your air fryer and give it a chance to shine. Making fried rice at home can be a challenge, and it just never tastes the same – but with an air fryer, you can get that amazingly crispy, lightly fried texture without buckets of oil, salt, and a costly food bill. It only takes about 20 minutes to toss this recipe together, and it tastes just like the real thing.

SERVES: 2

You will need:

- 2 cups of cooked rice
- 2 tablespoons of soy sauce
- 1 tablespoon of sesame oil
- 1 tablespoon of water
- 2 teaspoons of vegetable oil
- 1 large egg
- 140 g / 1 cup of thawed frozen peas
- 150 g / 1 cup of thawed frozen carrots
- 1 pinch of salt
- 1 pinch of black pepper

1 Get out a medium bowl and add the cooked rice, both kinds of oil, water, salt, and pepper, and stir them together.

2 Preheat your air fryer to 175 degrees C / 350 degrees F.

3 Tip the mixture into a round tin and place it in the air fryer basket.

4 Place it in the air fryer and cook for 5 minutes, and then take it out and stir.

5 Put it back in and cook it for another 5 minutes.

6 Beat the egg in a small bowl and pour it over the rice, and put it back in the fryer for another 4 minutes.

7 Check that the egg has set and stir in the thawed carrots and peas, breaking the egg into chunks.

8 Cook for another couple of minutes, and then serve steaming hot with soy sauce drizzled over the top.

Nutritional info:

Calories: 320

Fat: 14.3 g

Cholesterol: 93 mg

Sodium: 1111 mg

Carbohydrates: 38 g

Fibre: 6.2 g

Protein: 10.6 g

Air Fried Macaroni Cheese

You need a dish to make macaroni cheese in your air fryer, but if you have one, you'll probably never make it any other way again. This meal is creamy, cheesy, and delightfully crispy on the top, and you can make it in under half an hour. It creates a filling meal that will be loved by kids and adults alike. If you enjoy a bit of spice, try chopping some fresh chilli into the mix, or add a bit of smoky paprika.

SERVES: 4

You will need:

- 200 g / 1 1/2 cups of macaroni
- 530 ml / 2 1/4 cups of milk
- 240 g / 2 cups of grated cheddar
- Pinch of salt
- Pinch of pepper
- 1/4 teaspoon of ground nutmeg

1 Preheat your air fryer to 170 degrees C / 340 degrees F.

2 Take out a 7 cm deep dish that will fit into your air fryer.

3 Add the macaroni to the dish, followed by the milk, cheese, and seasoning, and stir well.

4 Place the dish in the air fryer basket and allow it to cook for 7 minutes. Take it out and mix it, making sure none of the pasta is sticking.

5 Put it back for another 7 minutes and then stir again.

6 Cook it for another 5 minutes and then test whether the pasta is to your liking. It can have another couple of minutes if you prefer it softer. Otherwise, take it out and allow it to stand for about 3 minutes, and then serve.

Nutritional info:

Calories: 414

Fat: 22.1 g

Cholesterol: 71 mg

Sodium: 456 mg

Carbohydrates: 31.1 g

Fibre: 1.1 g

Protein: 22.7 g

Air Fried Crunchy Mushrooms

Mushrooms are a highly versatile vegetable, and they can become an amazing main dish in your air fryer. You may want to add some potatoes or something alongside this, or have them with a bit of toast, but they are surprisingly filling as they are. This is a super simple vegetarian recipe that will let you enjoy a crispy coating without any chicken in sight.

SERVES: 2

You will need:

- 125 g / 2 cups (approximately) of oyster mushrooms
- 240 ml / 1 cup of buttermilk
- 200 g / 1 ½ cups of flour
- 1 teaspoon of salt
- 1 teaspoon of onion powder
- 1 teaspoon of smoked paprika
- 1 teaspoon of pepper
- 1 teaspoon of cumin
- 1 teaspoon garlic powder
- 1 tablespoon of oil

1 Wash the oyster mushrooms and pat them dry, and toss them into the buttermilk in a large bowl.

2 Leave it to sit for 15 minutes and then preheat your air fryer to 190 degrees C / 375 degrees F.

3 Take out a large bowl and combine the spices and the flour. Carefully lift each mushroom out of the buttermilk and dip it into the flour. Roll it around and then tap off the excess flour. Do this for each mushroom.

4 Dip the mushrooms back into the buttermilk, and then into flour to apply a second coating.

5 Get a pan that will fit in your air fryer, and grease it lightly.

6 Place the mushrooms in the pan in a single layer, leaving space between each for the air to circulate.

7 Cook the mushrooms for 5 minutes, and then take the basket out and lightly brush the mushrooms with some oil to help them brown.

(8) Put them back in the basket and check on them after another 5 minutes. If they are not yet golden, give them a further 3 to 5 minutes, and check that they are crispy and delicious. Serve them with any side of vegetables that you like; they go well with peas and potatoes. They are best eaten hot.

Nutritional info:

Calories: 489

Fat: 9.5 g

Cholesterol: 5 mg

Sodium: 1308 mg

Carbohydrates: 84.9 g

Fibre: 5 g

Protein: 16.6 g

Air Fried Scallops

For a fancy dinner where you're treating yourself, you can't go wrong with scallops, and these crispy, light scallops are perfect for a little luxury. Make them for a date night or a birthday, and they are bound to be enjoyed by everyone lucky enough to try them.

SERVES: 2

You will need:

- 🍽 900 g / 2 lb. of scallops
- 🍽 120 g / 1 cup of Italian breadcrumbs
- 🍽 1 teaspoon of garlic powder
- 🍽 1 teaspoon of black pepper
- 🍽 4 tablespoons of butter
- 🍽 ½ teaspoon of salt

Method:

1. Take out a shallow bowl and mix together the seasonings and breadcrumbs.

2. In a separate bowl, melt the butter.

3. Roll the scallops in the butter, and then in the breadcrumbs. They need to be fully coated; add more butter and give them a second swipe in the breadcrumbs if necessary.

4. Preheat your air fryer to 200 degrees C / 390 degrees F.

5. Lightly grease your air fryer basket and then add the scallops in a single layer. You may need to work in batches.

6. Fry the scallops for 2 minutes, and then flip them using tongs. Fry for 3 more minutes.

7. Take a scallop out and cut it open to check that it is opaque throughout. The breadcrumbs should have turned golden brown.

Nutritional info:

Calories: 823

Fat: 29.4 g

Cholesterol: 211 mg

Sodium: 1871 mg

Carbohydrates: 51.3 g

Fibre: 2.9 g

Protein: 83.9 g

Amber Garfield

Delicious Air Fryer Side Dishes

||||||||||||||||||||||||||||||||||||||||||||||||||||||||||||||||||||||||||||||||||||||||||

Your air fryer is also a great means of making side dishes, so if you're planning a dinner, don't underestimate its usefulness. You can create some inventive and unusual recipes, and many of these can be left to cook while you focus on the main meal. They are quick and easy, and make superb sides!

Green Bean And Mushroom Dish

Green beans are delicious, and mushrooms are filling and healthy – so put them together and you get magic in a bowl. This should only take about 20 minutes to make, and it's a tasty side that's a great way to boost your intake of vegetables. You can serve this with pretty much any meal, and they'll steal the show with their crunchy goodness.

SERVES: 6

You will need:

- 1 red onion (small)
- 2 tablespoons of olive oil
- 450 g / 1 lb of green beans
- 225 g / ½ lb of mushrooms
- Pinch of pepper
- Pinch of salt
- 1 teaspoon of Italian seasoning

Amber Garfield

1. Preheat your air fryer to 190 degrees C / 375 degrees F.

2. Wash the mushrooms and green beans.

3. Peel your red onion and slice it thinly.

4. Slice the mushrooms and cut the green beans into 2 inch pieces.

5. Lightly grease a tray.

6. Toss all the ingredients together, including the olive oil and the seasoning.

7. Put the ingredients on the tray and place it in the air fryer basket, and then cook for about 10 minutes.

8. Take the basket out and toss everything, and then cook for another 10 minutes. The vegetables should turn lightly golden. Serve hot and enjoy.

Nutritional info:

Calories: 79

Fat: 5.1 g

Cholesterol: 1 mg

Sodium: 104 mg

Carbohydrates: 7.8 g

Fibre: 3.2 g

Protein: 2.7 g

Amber Garfield

Sweet Potato Tots In The Air Fryer

If you love sweet potato tots but find that they are often a bit heavy for a side dish, your air fryer may be a great alternative. You can create a batch in a little over half an hour, and these tend to be immensely popular with kids, but loved by adults too. You can serve them with any dipping sauce you like, and they are a wonderful accompaniment to fish recipes, or a lovely side to pair with fried eggs and baked beans.

SERVES: 1 2 (2 TOTS EACH)

You will need:

- 🍴 260 g / 9 oz sweet potatoes
- 🍴 1/2 teaspoon of olive oil
- 🍴 Pinch of salt
- 🍴 Pinch of pepper
- 🍴 1/2 teaspoon of chilli powder

Method:

1. Wash your sweet potatoes and peel them if you would rather not include the skins in the recipe.

2. Bring a pan of water to the boil and boil the potatoes until they are tender but not mushy. This should take about 15 minutes. If you over-cook them, they will not grate well.

3. Drain the potatoes and allow them to cool.

4. Grate the potatoes and mix in the seasoning, and then shape the mixture into tots. You should get about 24 tots.

5. Preheat your air fryer to 200 degrees C / 400 degrees F.

6. Lightly grease your air fryer basket with the olive oil and then put the tots inside, leaving some space between each so that the air can circulate properly.

7. Brush a little olive oil over the tots and then cook them for 8 minutes. Use tongs to turn them over, brush the other side with oil, and cook them for another 8 minutes.

Amber Garfield

Nutritional info (per tot):

Calories: 28

Fat: 0.3 g

Cholesterol: 0 mg

Sodium: 14 mg

Carbohydrates: 6.1 g

Fibre: 1 g

Protein: 0.4 g

Cheesy Potatoes

If you want a seriously rich and tasty side that will pair well with almost anything, cheesy potatoes are a great choice. You can use sweet potatoes or just plain white potatoes if you prefer; either way, this dish is bursting with flavour and will prove popular at any mealtime. It can be served with chicken, fish, steak, or any vegetable dish that you like.

SERVES: 4

You will need:

- 1 medium sweet potato
- 1 medium white potato
- 1 teaspoon of thyme
- 3 cloves of garlic
- 240 ml / 1 cup of reduced fat milk
- 40 g / ¼ cup of onion
- 125 g / 1 ¼ cups of mozzarella
- Pinch of salt
- Pinch of pepper
- 25 g / ¼ cup of Parmesan

Amber Garfield

1. Wash and slice the white potato and sweet potato into the thinnest slices you can achieve.

2. Coat a round baking tray with oil and then add one layer of potato around the base.

3. Peel and slice the garlic as finely as you can, and add this on top of the potato, with some of the mozzarella and the seasoning.

4. Repeat the process, alternating the sweet potato with the white potato, and then adding the seasoning on top of the layer. Keep doing this until you have used all of the potato.

5. Press it down firmly and pour the milk over the top. Preheat your air fryer to 175 degrees C / 350 degrees F.

6. Cover the tray with aluminium foil and then put it in the air fryer and bake it for 40 minutes.

7. Take it out, remove the foil, and use a knife to check that the potatoes are tender. Sprinkle any remaining mozzarella on the top, along with the grated Parmesan.

8. Increase the air fryer temperature to 200 degrees C / 400 degrees F and then cook for a further 5 minutes to turn the topping golden. Serve hot.

Nutritional info:

Calories: 142

Fat: 4.3 g

Cholesterol: 2.6 g

Sodium: 444 mg

Carbohydrates: 18.6 g

Fibre: 2.3 g

Protein: 8.2 g

Bacon-Wrapped Asparagus

If you love bacon and you want to bring some elegance to your dinner, these simple asparagus spears are a wonderful way to do it. You need to get really fresh asparagus for the best results, but these are easy to make, popular, and very tasty. They also look pretty when served on a plate.

SERVES: 4

You will need:

- 12 slices of bacon
- 24 stalks of asparagus
- 1/2 teaspoon of oil
- 1/2 teaspoon of black pepper

Method:

1 Take your slices of bacon and some scissors, and cut each slice down the length to make thinner strips.

2 Cut the ends off the asparagus spears.

3 Lightly oil the basket of the air fryer to stop the spears from sticking and preheat your air fryer to 200 degrees C / 390 degrees F.

4 Take one stalk of asparagus and one half bacon slice, and wrap the bacon around the stalk in a spiral.

5 Place the stalk in the basket, and do the same for the other stalks. Make sure that there are gaps between each one once they are in the basket. You may need to work in batches.

6 Roast the stalks for about 5 minutes, and then take the basket out and turn each one to expose a new side. Roast for another 5 minutes, until the bacon is crispy and the stalks are tender.

7 Sprinkle the asparagus with ground pepper and serve hot.

Nutritional info:

Calories: 333

Fat: 24.5 g

Cholesterol: 63 mg

Sodium: 1319 mg

Carbohydrates: 4.7 g

Fibre: 2.1 g

Protein: 23.3 g

Air Fried Tortilla Chips

Anyone who loves tortilla chips will instantly fall for this delicious recipe, which creates crunchy crisps that can be flavoured in any way that you prefer. Forget all the unpleasant ingredients that end up in commercial chips – you're in full control here, and this simple recipe only takes about 20 minutes to put together. If you're serving a buffet or settling down for a movie, these are the perfect snack, and much healthier than crisps / chips that have been deep fried! The recipe given here is for salt and vinegar, but you can easily add a bit of spice, some cheese, or sweet flavourings for a dessert-like twist.

SERVES: 3 (24 CHIPS)

You will need:

- ½ teaspoon of vinegar
- 1 tablespoon of olive oil
- 1 teaspoon of salt
- 6 corn tortillas

Method:

1. Whisk the olive oil, salt, and vinegar in a small bowl until fully combined.

2. Preheat your air fryer to 175 degrees C / 350 degrees F.

3. Lightly brush both sides of your tortillas with the mixture and then cut each tortilla in half and then half again so you get neat triangles that can easily be eaten.

4. Arrange a single layer of the tortillas in the air fryer basket and put the basket in the fryer.

5. Cook for about 8 minutes and then check whether they are crispy enough. Tip them out onto a wire rack and start the next batch.

6. When the chips are all cooked, allow them to cool completely, and transfer them to an airtight container or eat them straight away.

Nutritional info (per chip):

Calories: 145

Fat: 6 g

Cholesterol: 0 mg

Sodium: 797 mg

Carbohydrates: 21.5 g

Fibre: 3 g

Protein: 2.7 g

Conclusion

Cooking with an air fryer can be an amazing experience, and if you are keen to have a go, hopefully these recipes will give you the success and enjoyment that you need. Making air fryer recipes is a great way to cut fats out of your diet and eat healthier foods, and it's also a means of injecting new energy into your cooking so that it becomes more fun. You can make all sorts of creative things in your air fryer, so don't limit yourself to a bit of bacon and some chips / fries when you fancy a meal.

Whether you are cooking vegetables, meat, fish, sides, or desserts, your air fryer is a great tool that you should be utilising at every opportunity, so make the most of it and don't be afraid to experiment. Remember to use the tips from the start of this book to ensure that you are making the most of your air fryer and cooking the best food possible.

EXCLUSIVE BONUS

40 Weight Loss Recipes

&

14 Days Meal Plan

Scan the QR-Code and receive
the FREE download:

Disclaimer

This book contains opinions and ideas of the author and is meant to teach the reader informative and helpful knowledge while due care should be taken by the user in the application of the information provided. The instructions and strategies are possibly not right for every reader and there is no guarantee that they work for everyone. Using this book and implementing the information/recipes therein contained is explicitly your own responsibility and risk. This work with all its contents, does not guarantee correctness, completion, quality or correctness of the provided information. Misinformation or misprints cannot be completely eliminated.

Printed in Great Britain
by Amazon

13109218R00064